WHAT IS
CHRISTMAS?

Elaine Landau

Enslow Elementary
an imprint of
Enslow Publishers, Inc.
40 Industrial Road
Box 398
Berkeley Heights, NJ 07922
USA
http://www.enslow.com

CONTENTS

WORDS TO KNOW

carol (KA ruhl)—A song of praise or joy. Some Christmas carols celebrate the birth of Jesus.

choir (KWYE ur)—A group of singers who sing together. Many churches have choirs.

Christian (KRIS chin)— A person who believes in Jesus and follows his teachings.

3

A SPECIAL
DAY
IS COMING

Children write lists for Santa Claus.
People sing carols. They mail cards
to their friends. Lights are hung
on trees. What time of year is this?
It must be Christmas time!

AN IMPORTANT
TIME

Christmas is December 25. Christians celebrate the birth of Jesus. They believe He is the son of God. For four weeks before Christmas, they get ready. They light candles on a wreath.

The last candle on an Advent wreath is lit on the Sunday before Christmas.

SO MUCH TO DO

Lots of homes have Christmas trees. People hang lights and shiny balls on the branches. They bake cookies. They make or buy presents. They wrap the presents in pretty paper.

CONCERTS AND PLAYS

Some schools have Christmas concerts. Children play music and sing. They may act out a play. Some classes have parties. Children may dress up as candy canes!

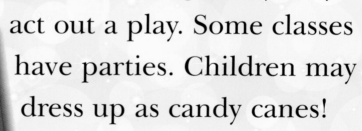

CHILDREN WAIT FOR SANTA

Kids wait for Santa on Christmas Eve. Some leave cookies for him. They hope he brings them toys. Children hang up stockings, too. Will these be filled with treats?

CHRISTMAS DAY AT
CHURCH

Many people go to church. They pray for peace on earth. They hear the story of the birth of Jesus. Church choirs sing songs. Everyone feels the joy of Christmas.

A DAY FOR
FAMILY AND
FRIENDS

People come from near and far to be together. They sing songs. They give each other gifts and hugs. Some cook large dinners. There may be turkey, fish, vegetables, or pasta.

A TIME FOR
GIVING

People help those who have less.
They bring food, blankets, and
clothes to those who need them.
It feels special to help one
another at Christmas.

A FUN CHRISTMAS CRAFT

This year have your Christmas tree look better than ever. Make a popcorn and cranberry string to hang on it!

You Will Need:

- ❖ large bag of air-popped popcorn
- ❖ sewing needle
- ❖ waxed dental floss
- ❖ bag of fresh cranberries

What to Do:

1. Tie a knot at one end of a dental floss string.

2. Ask an adult to thread the other end through a needle.

3. Ask an adult to help you put the needle through a cranberry and push it to the end of the string.

4. Do the same with a piece of popcorn.

5. Repeat until the dental floss string is nearly filled with cranberries and popcorn.

6. Leave a few inches at the top of the string and knot it.

7. Place the string on your Christmas tree where you think it will look best.

8. When the tree comes down, do not throw your popcorn and cranberry string away. Take the popcorn and berries off the string. Toss them in your yard or park. It will be a late Christmas gift for the birds!

LEARN MORE

BOOKS

Butler, Dori Hillestad. *Christmas: Season of Peace and Joy*. Mankato, Minn.: Capstone Press, 2007.

Dowly, Tim. *My First Story of Christmas*. Chicago: Moody Publishers, 2004.

Stevens, Kathryn. *Christmas Trees*. Mankato, Minn.: The Child's World, 2010.

Trueit, Trudi Strain. *Christmas*. Tarrytown, N.Y.: Marshall Cavendish Corp., 2010.

WEB SITES

Reindeer Word Search

http://www.kidsturncentral.com/games/wsearchc2.htm

Christmas Jigsaw Puzzle

http://www.dltk-holidays.com/xmas/puzzles/6.htm

INDEX

Enslow Elementary, an imprint of Enslow Publishers, Inc.

Enslow Elementary® is a registered trademark of Enslow Publishers, Inc.

Copyright © 2012 by Elaine Landau

Library of Congress Cataloging-in-Publication Data

Landau, Elaine.
  What is Christmas? / by Elaine Landau.
    p. cm. — (I like holidays!)
  Includes index.
  Summary: "An introduction to Christmas with an easy activity"— Provided by publisher.
  ISBN 978-0-7660-3702-1
  1. Christmas—Juvenile literature. I. Title.
  GT4985.5.L34 2012
  394.2663—dc22   2010039476

Paperback ISBN 978-1-59845-295-2

Printed in China

052011 Leo Paper Group, Heshan City, Guangdong, China

10 9 8 7 6 5 4 3 2 1

Photo Credits: Alamy: © Corbis Premium RF, p. 11; © Frances Roberts, p. 3 (choir); © Michael Newman/PhotoEdit, p. 10; Associated Press, p. 19; iStockphoto.com: © Alex Slobodkin, p. 6, © Carmen Martínez Banús, p. 12; © Paul Tessier, p. 20, © Sean Locke, p. 8; Photo Library: © Andersen Ross, p. 21, © Godong Godong, p. 15, © Hill Street Studios, p. 4 (inset); Shutterstock.com, pp. 1, 2, 3 (Christian), 4, 7, 16, 17, 22, 23, 24.

Cover Photo: Shutterstock.com

Series Consultant:
Duncan R. Jamieson, PhD
Professor of History
Ashland University
Ashland, OH

Series Literacy Consultant:
Allan A. De Fina, PhD
Dean, College of Education/Professor of
    Literacy Education
New Jersey City University
Past President of the New Jersey Reading Association